Alfred Tennyson

Demeter and Other Poems

Alfred Tennyson

Demeter and Other Poems

ISBN/EAN: 9783337006075

Printed in Europe, USA, Canada, Australia, Japan

Cover: Foto ©Thomas Meinert / pixelio.de

More available books at **www.hansebooks.com**

DEMETER

AND OTHER POEMS

BY

ALFRED
LORD TENNYSON

D.C.L. P.L.

London
MACMILLAN AND CO.
AND NEW YORK
1889

All rights reserved

CONTENTS

	PAGE
TO THE MARQUIS OF DUFFERIN AND AVA	1
ON THE JUBILEE OF QUEEN VICTORIA	6
TO PROFESSOR JEBB	12
DEMETER AND PERSEPHONE	14
OWD ROÄ	24
VASTNESS	41
THE RING	48
FORLORN	85
HAPPY	93
TO ULYSSES	111
TO MARY BOYLE	117
THE PROGRESS OF SPRING	123
MERLIN AND THE GLEAM	132
ROMNEY'S REMORSE	142
PARNASSUS	153

	PAGE
By an Evolutionist	157
Far—far—away	161
Politics	163
Beautiful City	164
The Roses on the Terrace	165
The Play	166
On One who affected an Effeminate Manner	166
To One who ran down the English	167
The Snowdrop	168
The Throstle	169
The Oak	171
In Memoriam—William George Ward	173
Crossing the Bar	174

ERRATA.

p. 4, line 6, *for* The was, *read* the Was
p. 117, line 6, *for* one *read* our
p. 150, line 9, *for* More than *read* Than

TO THE MARQUIS OF DUFFERIN AND AVA.

I.

At times our Britain cannot rest,
    At times her steps are swift and rash;
    She moving, at her girdle clash
The golden keys of East and West.

II.

Not swift or rash, when late she lent
    The sceptres of her West, her East,
    To one, that ruling has increased
Her greatness and her self-content.

III.

Your rule has made the people love
    Their ruler. Your viceregal days
    Have added fulness to the phrase
Of 'Gauntlet in the velvet glove.'

IV.

But since your name will grow with Time,
    Not all, as honouring your fair fame
    Of Statesman, have I made the name
A golden portal to my rhyme:

V.

But more, that you and yours may know
    From me and mine, how dear a debt
    We owed you, and are owing yet
To you and yours, and still would owe.

VI.

For he—your India was his Fate,

    And drew him over sea to you—

    He fain had ranged her thro' and thro',

To serve her myriads and the State,—

VII.

A soul that, watch'd from earliest youth,

    And on thro' many a brightening year,

    Had never swerved for craft or fear,

By one side-path, from simple truth;

VIII.

Who might have chased and claspt Renown

    And caught her chaplet here—and there

    In haunts of jungle-poison'd air

The flame of life went wavering down;

IX.

But ere he left your fatal shore,
    And lay on that funereal boat,
    Dying, 'Unspeakable' he wrote
'Their kindness,' and he wrote no more;

X.

And sacred is the latest word;
    And now The was, the Might-have-been,
    And those lone rites I have not seen,
And one drear sound I have not heard,

XI.

Are dreams that scarce will let me be,
    Not there to bid my boy farewell,
    When That within the coffin fell
Fell and flash'd into the Red Sea,

XII.

Beneath a hard Arabian moon

    And alien stars.   To question, why

    The sons before the fathers die,

Not mine! and I may meet him soon;

XIII.

But while my life's late eve endures,

    Nor settles into hueless gray,

    My memories of his briefer day

Will mix with love for you and yours.

ON THE JUBILEE OF QUEEN VICTORIA.

I.

Fifty times the rose has flower'd and faded,

Fifty times the golden harvest fallen,

Since our Queen assumed the globe, the sceptre.

II.

She beloved for a kindliness

Rare in Fable or History,

Queen, and Empress of India,

Crown'd so long with a diadem

Never worn by a worthier,

Now with prosperous auguries

Comes at last to the bounteous

Crowning year of her Jubilee.

III.

Nothing of the lawless, of the Despot,

Nothing of the vulgar, or vainglorious,

All is gracious, gentle, great and Queenly.

IV.

You then joyfully, all of you,

Set the mountain aflame to-night,

Shoot your stars to the firmament,

Deck your houses, illuminate

All your towns for a festival,

And in each let a multitude

Loyal, each, to the heart of it,

One full voice of allegiance,

Hail the fair Ceremonial

Of this year of her Jubilee.

v.

Queen, as true to womanhood as Queenhood,

Glorying in the glories of her people,

Sorrowing with the sorrows of the lowest!

vi.

You, that wanton in affluence,

Spare not now to be bountiful,

Call your poor to regale with you,

All the lowly, the destitute,

Make their neighbourhood healthfuller,

Give your gold to the Hospital,

Let the weary be comforted,

Let the needy be banqueted,

Let the maim'd in his heart rejoice

At this glad Ceremonial,

And this year of her Jubilee.

VII.

Henry's fifty years are all in shadow,

Gray with distance Edward's fifty summers,

Ev'n her Grandsire's fifty half forgotten.

VIII.

You, the Patriot Architect,

You that shape for Eternity,

Raise a stately memorial,

Make it regally gorgeous,

Some Imperial Institute,

Rich in symbol, in ornament,

Which may speak to the centuries,

All the centuries after us,

Of this great Ceremonial,

And this year of her Jubilee.

IX.

Fifty years of ever-broadening Commerce!

Fifty years of ever-brightening Science!

Fifty years of ever-widening Empire!

X.

You, the Mighty, the Fortunate,

You, the Lord-territorial,

You, the Lord-manufacturer,

You, the hardy, laborious,

Patient children of Albion,

You, Canadian, Indian,

Australasian, African,

All your hearts be in harmony,

All your voices in unison,

Singing 'Hail to the glorious

Golden year of her Jubilee!'

XI.

Are there thunders moaning in the distance?

Are there spectres moving in the darkness?

Trust the Hand of Light will lead her people,

Till the thunders pass, the spectres vanish,

And the Light is Victor, and the darkness

Dawns into the Jubilee of the Ages.

TO PROFESSOR JEBB,

WITH THE FOLLOWING POEM.

FAIR things are slow to fade away,

Bear witness you, that yesterday [1]

    From out the Ghost of Pindar in you

Roll'd an Olympian; and they say [2]

That here the torpid mummy wheat

Of Egypt bore a grain as sweet

    As that which gilds the glebe of England,

Sunn'd with a summer of milder heat.

[1] In Bologna.   [2] They say, for the fact is doubtful.

So may this legend for awhile,

If greeted by your classic smile,

    Tho' dead in its Trinacrian Enna,

Blossom again on a colder isle.

DEMETER AND PERSEPHONE.

(In Enna.)

Faint as a climate-changing bird that flies

All night across the darkness, and at dawn

Falls on the threshold of her native land,

And can no more, thou camest, O my child,

Led upward by the God of ghosts and dreams,

Who laid thee at Eleusis, dazed and dumb

With passing thro' at once from state to state,

Until I brought thee hither, that the day,

When here thy hands let fall the gather'd flower,

Might break thro' clouded memories once again

On thy lost self.   A sudden nightingale

Saw thee, and flash'd into a frolic of song

And welcome; and a gleam as of the moon,

When first she peers along the tremulous deep,

Fled wavering o'er thy face, and chased away

That shadow of a likeness to the king

Of shadows, thy dark mate.   Persephone!

Queen of the dead no more—my child! Thine
    eyes

Again were human-godlike, and the Sun

Burst from a swimming fleece of winter gray,

And robed thee in his day from head to feet—

'Mother!' and I was folded in thine arms.

    Child, those imperial, disimpassion'd, eyes

Awed even me at first, thy mother—eyes

That oft had seen the serpent-wanded power

Draw downward into Hades with his drift
Of flickering spectres, lighted from below
By the red race of fiery Phlegethon;
But when before have Gods or men beheld
The Life that had descended re-arise,
And lighted from above him by the Sun?
So mighty was the mother's childless cry,
A cry that rang thro' Hades, Earth, and Heaven!

So in this pleasant vale we stand again,
The field of Enna, now once more ablaze
With flowers that brighten as thy footstep falls,
All flowers—but for one black blur of earth
Left by that closing chasm, thro' which the car
Of dark Aïdoneus rising rapt thee hence.
And here, my child, tho' folded in thine arms,
I feel the deathless heart of motherhood

Within me shudder, lest the naked glebe

Should yawn once more into the gulf, and thence

The shrilly whinnyings of the team of Hell,

Ascending, pierce the glad and songful air,

And all at once their arch'd necks, midnight-maned,

Jet upward thro' the mid-day blossom. No!

For, see, thy foot has touch'd it; all the space

Of blank earth-baldness clothes itself afresh,

And breaks into the crocus-purple hour

That saw thee vanish.

                    Child, when thou wert gone,

I envied human wives, and nested birds,

Yea, the cubb'd lioness; went in search of thee

Thro' many a palace, many a cot, and gave

Thy breast to ailing infants in the night,

And set the mother waking in amaze

To find her sick one whole; and forth again
Among the wail of midnight winds, and cried,
'Where is my loved one? Wherefore do ye wail?'
And out from all the night an answer shrill'd,
'We know not, and we know not why we wail.'
I climb'd on all the cliffs of all the seas,
And ask'd the waves that moan about the world
'Where? do ye make your moaning for my child?'
And round from all the world the voices came
'We know not, and we know not why we moan.'
'Where'? and I stared from every eagle-peak,
I thridded the black heart of all the woods,
I peer'd thro' tomb and cave, and in the storms
Of Autumn swept across the city, and heard
The murmur of their temples chanting me,
Me, me, the desolate Mother! 'Where'?—and
  turn'd,

And fled by many a waste, forlorn of man,
And grieved for man thro' all my grief for thee,—
The jungle rooted in his shatter'd hearth,
The serpent coil'd about his broken shaft,
The scorpion crawling over naked skulls;—
I saw the tiger in the ruin'd fane
Spring from his fallen God, but trace of thee
I saw not; and far on, and, following out
A league of labyrinthine darkness, came
On three gray heads beneath a gleaming rift.
'Where'? and I heard one voice from all the three
'We know not, for we spin the lives of men,
And not of Gods, and know not why we spin!
There is a Fate beyond us.' Nothing knew.

   Last as the likeness of a dying man,
Without his knowledge, from him flits to warn

A far-off friendship that he comes no more,
So he, the God of dreams, who heard my cry,
Drew from thyself the likeness of thyself
Without thy knowledge, and thy shadow past
Before me, crying 'The Bright one in the highest
Is brother of the Dark one in the lowest,
And Bright and Dark have sworn that I, the child
Of thee, the great Earth-Mother, thee, the Power
That lifts her buried life from gloom to bloom,
Should be for ever and for evermore
The Bride of Darkness.'

       So the Shadow wail'd.
Then I, Earth-Goddess, cursed the Gods of Heaven.
I would not mingle with their feasts; to me
Their nectar smack'd of hemlock on the lips,
Their rich ambrosia tasted aconite.

The man, that only lives and loves an hour,
Seem'd nobler than their hard Eternities.
My quick tears kill'd the flower, my ravings hush'd
The bird, and lost in utter grief I fail'd
To send my life thro' olive-yard and vine
And golden grain, my gift to helpless man.
Rain-rotten died the wheat, the barley-spears
Were hollow-husk'd, the leaf fell, and the sun,
Pale at my grief, drew down before his time
Sickening, and Ætna kept her winter snow.

    Then He, the brother of this Darkness, He
Who still is highest, glancing from his height
On earth a fruitless fallow, when he miss'd
The wonted steam of sacrifice, the praise
And prayer of men, decreed that thou should'st dwell
For nine white moons of each whole year with me,
Three dark ones in the shadow with thy King.

Once more the reaper in the gleam of dawn
Will see me by the landmark far away,
Blessing his field, or seated in the dusk
Of even, by the lonely threshing-floor,
Rejoicing in the harvest and the grange.

Yet I, Earth-Goddess, am but ill-content
With them, who still are highest. Those gray heads,
What meant they by their 'Fate beyond the Fates'
But younger kindlier Gods to bear us down,
As we bore down the Gods before us? Gods,
To quench, not hurl the thunderbolt, to stay,
Not spread the plague, the famine; Gods indeed,
To send the noon into the night and break
The sunless halls of Hades into Heaven?
Till thy dark lord accept and love the Sun,
And all the Shadow die into the Light,

When thou shalt dwell the whole bright year with
 me,
And souls of men, who grew beyond their race,
And made themselves as Gods against the fear
Of Death and Hell; and thou that hast from men,
As Queen of Death, that worship which is Fear,
Henceforth, as having risen from out the dead,
Shalt ever send thy life along with mine
From buried grain thro' springing blade, and bless
Their garner'd Autumn also, reap with me,
Earth-mother, in the harvest hymns of Earth
The worship which is Love, and see no more
The Stone, the Wheel, the dimly-glimmering lawns
Of that Elysium, all the hateful fires
Of torment, and the shadowy warrior glide
Along the silent field of Asphodel.

OWD ROÄ.[1]

Naäy, noä mander[2] o' use to be callin' 'im Roä, Roä, Roä,

Fo' the dog's stoän-deäf, an' e's blind, 'e can neither stan' nor goä.

But I meäns fur to maäke 'is owd aäge as 'appy as iver I can,

Fur I owäs owd Roäver moor nor I iver owäd mottal man.

Thou's rode of 'is back when a babby, afoor thou was gotten too owd,

For 'e'd fetch an' carry like owt, 'e was allus as good as gowd.

Eh, but 'e'd fight wi' a will *when* 'e fowt; 'e could howd³ 'is oan,
An' Roä was the dog as knaw'd when an' wheere to bury his boane.

An' 'e kep his heäd hoop like a king, an' 'e'd niver not down wi' 'is täail,
Fur 'e'd niver done nowt to be shäamed on, when we was i' Howlaby Daäle.

An' 'e sarved me sa well when 'e lived, that, Dick, when 'e cooms to be deäd,
I thinks as I'd like fur to hev soom soort of a sarvice reäd.

Fur 'e's moor good sense na the Parliament man 'at stans fur us 'ere,
An' I'd voät fur 'im, my oän sen, if 'e could but stan fur the Shere.

'Faäithful an' True'—them words be i' Scriptur—
an' Faäithful an' True
Ull be fun'[4] upo' four short legs ten times fur one upo' two.

An' maäybe they'll walk upo' two but I knaws they runs upo' four,[5]—
Bedtime, Dicky! but waäit till tha 'eärs it be strikin' the hour.

Fur I wants to tell tha o' Roä when we lived i' Howlaby Daäle,
Ten year sin—Naäy—naäy! tha mun nobbut hev' one glass of aäle.

Straänge an' owd-farran'd[6] the 'ouse, an' belt[7] long afoor my daäy
Wi' haäfe o' the chimleys a-twizzen'd[8] an' twined like a band o' haäy.

The fellers as maäkes them picturs, 'ud coom at the fall o' the year,
An' sattle their ends upo stools to pictur the door-poorch theere,

An' the Heagle 'as hed two heäds stannin' theere o' the brokken stick;[9]
An' they niver 'ed seed sich ivin'[10] as graw'd hall ower the brick;

An' theere i' the 'ouse one night—but it's down, an' all on it now
Goan into mangles an' tonups,[11] an' raäved slick thruf by the plow—

Theere, when the 'ouse wur a house, one night I wur sittin' aloän,
Wi' Roäver athurt my feeät, an' sleeäpin still as a stoän,

Of a Christmas Eäve, an' as cowd as this, an' the
  midders [12] as white,
An' the fences all on 'em bolster'd oop wi' the
  windle [13] that night;

An' the cat wur a-sleeäpin alongside Roäver, but I
  wur awaäke,
An' smoäkin' an' thinkin' o' things—Doänt maäke
  thysen sick wi' the caäke.

Fur the men ater supper 'ed sung their songs an'
  'ed 'ed their beer,
An' 'ed goän their waäys; ther was nobbut three,
  an' noän on 'em theere.

They was all on 'em fear'd o' the Ghoäst an' dussn't
  not sleeäp i' the 'ouse,
But Dicky, the Ghoäst moästlins [14] was nobbut a
  rat or a mouse.

An' I looökt out wonst [15] at the night, an' the daäle
 was all of a thaw,
Fur I seed the beck coomin' down like a long black
 snaäke i' the snaw,
An' I heärd greät heäps o' the snaw slushin' down
 fro' the bank to the beck,
An' then as I stood i' the doorwaäy, I feeäld it
 drip o' my neck.

Saw I turn'd in ageän, an' I thowt o' the good owd
 times 'at was goan,
An' the munney they maäde by the war, an' the
 times 'at was coomin' on;

Fur I thowt if the Staäte was a gawin' to let in
 furriners wheät,
Howiver was British farmers to stan' ageän o' their
 feeät.

Howiver was I fur to find my rent an' to paäy my men?
An' all along o' the feller[16] as turn'd 'is back of hissen.

Thou slep i' the chaumber above us, we couldn't ha' 'eärd tha call,
Sa Moother 'ed tell'd ma to bring tha down, an' thy craädle an' all;

Fur the gell o' the farm 'at slep wi' tha then 'ed gotten wer leäve,
Fur to goä that night to 'er foälk by cause o' the Christmas Eäve;

But I cleän forgot tha, my lad, when Moother 'ed gotten to bed,
An' I slep i' my chair hup-on-end, an' the Freeä Traäde runn'd i' my 'ead,

Till I dreäm'd 'at Squire walkt in, an' I says to him
'Squire, ya're laäte,'
Then I seed at 'is faäce wur as red as the Yule-
block theer i' the graäte.

An' 'e says 'can ya paäy me the rent to-night?'
an' I says to 'im 'Noä,'
An' 'e cotch'd howd hard o' my hairm,[17] 'Then hout
to-night tha shall goä.'

'Tha'll niver,' says I, 'be a-turnin ma hout upo'
Christmas Eäve'?
Then I waäked an' I fun it was Roäver a-tuggin'
an' teärin' my slieäve.

An' I thowt as 'e'd goän cleän-wud,[18] fur I noäwaeys
knaw'd 'is intent;
An' I says 'Git awaäy, ya beäst,' an' I fetcht 'im a
kick an' 'e went.

Then 'e tummled up stairs, fur I 'eärd 'im, as if 'e'd 'a brokken 'is neck,
An' I'd cleär forgot, little Dicky, thy chaumber door wouldn't sneck;[19]

An' I slep' i' my chair ageän wi' my hairm hingin' down to the floor,
An' I thowt it was Roäver a-tuggin' an' teärin' me wuss nor afoor,

An' I thowt 'at I kick'd 'im ageän, but I kick'd thy Moother istead.
'What arta snorin' theere fur? the house is afire,' she said.

Thy Moother 'ed beän a-naggin' about the gell o' the farm,
She offens 'ud spy summut wrong when there warn't not a mossel o' harm;

An' she didn't not solidly meän I wur gawin' that
    waäy to the bad,
Fur the gell [20] was as howry a trollope as iver
    traäpes'd i' the squad.

But Moother was free of 'er tongue, as I offens 'ev
    tell'd 'er mysen,
Sa I kep i' my chair, fur I thowt she was nobbut a-
    rilin' ma then.

An' I says 'I'd be good to tha, Bess, if tha'd ony-
    waäys let ma be good,'
But she skelpt ma haäfe ower i' the chair, an'
    screeäd like a Howl gone wud [21]—

'Ya mun run fur the lether.[22] Git oop, if ya're
    onywaäys good for owt.'
And I says 'If I beänt noäwaäys—not nowadaäys
    —good fur nowt—

Yit I beänt sich a Nowt[23] of all Nowts as 'ull
hallus do as 'e's bid.'
'But the stairs is afire,' she said; then I seed 'er
a-cryin', I did.

An' she beäld 'Ya mun saäve little Dick, an' be
sharp about it an' all,'
Sa I runs to the yard fur a lether, an' sets 'im ageän
the wall,

An' I claums an' I mashes the winder hin, when I
gits to the top,
But the heät druv hout i' my heyes till I feäld
mysen ready to drop.

Thy Moother was howdin' the lether, an' tellin' me
not to be skeärd,
An' I wasn't afeärd, or I thinks leästwaäys as I
wasn't afeärd;

But I couldn't see fur the smoäke wheere thou was
a-liggin, my lad,
An' Roäver was theere i' the chaumber a-yowlin' an'
yaupin' like mad;

An' thou was a-beälin' likewise, an' a-squeälin', as if
tha was bit,
An' it wasn't a bite but a burn, fur the merk's [24] o'
thy shou'der yit;

Then I call'd out Roä, Roä, Roä, thaw I didn't
haäfe think as 'e'd 'ear,
*But 'e coom'd thruf the fire wi' my bairn i' 'is
mouth to the winder theere!*

He coom'd like a Hangel o' marcy as soon as 'e
'eärd 'is naäme,
Or like tother Hangel i' Scriptur 'at summun seed
i' the flaäme,

When summun 'ed hax'd fur a son, an' 'e promised a son to she,
An' Roä was as good as the Hangel i' saävin' a son fur me.

Sa I browt tha down, an' I says 'I mun gaw up ageän fur Roä.'
'Gaw up ageän fur the varmint?' I tell'd 'er 'Yeäs I mun goä.'

An' I claumb'd up ageän to the winder, an' clemm'd [25] owd Roä by the 'eäd,
An' 'is 'air coom'd off i' my 'ands an' I taäked 'im at fust fur deäd;

Fur 'e smell'd like a herse a-singein', an' seeäm'd as blind as a poop,
An' haäfe on 'im bare as a bublin'.[26] I couldn't wakken 'im oop,

But I browt 'im down, an' we got to the barn, fur the barn wouldn't burn
Wi' the wind blawin' hard tother waäy, an' the wind wasn't like to turn.

An' *I* kep a-callin' o' Roä till 'e waggled 'is taäil fur a bit,
But the cocks kep a-crawin' an' crawin' all night, an' I 'ears 'em yit;

An' the dogs was a-yowlin' all round, and thou was a-squeälin' thysen,
An' Moother was naggin' an' groänin an' moänin' an' naggin' ageän;

An' I 'eärd the bricks an' the baulks[27] rummle down when the roof gev waäy,
Fur the fire was a-raägin' an' raävin' an' roarin' like judgment daäy.

Warm enew theere sewer-ly, but the barn was as cowd as owt,

An' we cuddled and huddled togither, an' happt [28] wersens oop as we mowt.

An' I browt Roä round, but Moother 'ed beän sa soäk'd wi' the thaw

'At she cotch'd 'er death o' cowd that night, poor soul, i' the straw.

Haäfe o' the parish runn'd oop when the rigtree [29] was tummlin' in—

Too laäte—but it's all ower now—hall hower—an' ten year sin;

Too laäte, tha mun git tha to bed, but I'll coom an' I'll squench the light,

Fur we moänt 'ev naw moor fires—and soa little Dick, good-night.

NOTES TO OWD ROÄ.

1 Old Rover.
2 Manner.
3 Hold.
4 Found.
5 'Ou' as in 'house.'
6 'Owd-farran'd,' old-fashioned.
7 Built.
8 'Twizzen'd,' twisted.
9 On a staff *raguté*.
10 Ivy.
11 Mangolds and turnips.
12 Meadows.
13 Drifted snow.
14 'Moästlins,' for the most part, generally.
15 Once.
16 Peel.
17 Arm.

[18] Mad.

[19] Latch.

[20] The girl was as dirty a slut as ever trudged in the mud, but there is a sense of slatternliness in 'traäpes'd' which is not expressed in 'trudged.'

[21] She half overturned me and shrieked like an owl gone mad.

[22] Ladder.

[23] A thoroughly insignificant or worthless person.

[24] Mark.

[25] Clutched.

[26] 'Bubbling,' a young unfledged bird.

[27] Beams.

[28] Wrapt ourselves.

[29] The beam that runs along the roof of the house just beneath the ridge.

VASTNESS.

I.

Many a hearth upon our dark globe sighs after many a vanish'd face,
Many a planet by many a sun may roll with the dust of a vanish'd race.

II.

Raving politics, never at rest—as this poor earth's pale history runs,—
What is it all but a trouble of ants in the gleam of a million million of suns?

III.

Lies upon this side, lies upon that side, truthless violence mourn'd by the Wise,

Thousands of voices drowning his own in a popular torrent of lies upon lies;

IV.

Stately purposes, valour in battle, glorious annals of army and fleet,

Death for the right cause, death for the wrong cause, trumpets of victory, groans of defeat;

V.

Innocence seethed in her mother's milk, and Charity setting the martyr aflame;

Thraldom who walks with the banner of Freedom, and recks not to ruin a realm in her name.

VI.

Faith at her zenith, or all but lost in the gloom of
    doubts that darken the schools;
Craft with a bunch of all-heal in her hand, follow'd
    up by her vassal legion of fools;

VII.

Trade flying over a thousand seas with her spice
    and her vintage, her silk and her corn;
Desolate offing, sailorless harbours, famishing
    populace, wharves forlorn;

VIII.

Star of the morning, Hope in the sunrise; gloom
    of the evening, Life at a close;
Pleasure who flaunts on her wide down-way with
    her flying robe and her poison'd rose;

IX.

Pain, that has crawl'd from the corpse of Pleasure,

    a worm which writhes all day, and at night

Stirs up again in the heart of the sleeper, and stings

    him back to the curse of the light;

X.

Wealth with his wines and his wedded harlots;

    honest Poverty, bare to the bone;

Opulent Avarice, lean as Poverty; Flattery gilding

    the rift in a throne;

XI.

Fame blowing out from her golden trumpet a

    jubilant challenge to Time and to Fate;

Slander, her shadow, sowing the nettle on all the

    laurel'd graves of the Great;

XII.

Love for the maiden, crown'd with marriage, no regrets for aught that has been,
Household happiness, gracious children, debtless competence, golden mean;

XIII.

National hatreds of whole generations, and pigmy spites of the village spire;
Vows that will last to the last death-ruckle, and vows that are snapt in a moment of fire;

XIV.

He that has lived for the lust of the minute, and died in the doing it, flesh without mind;
He that has nail'd all flesh to the Cross, till Self died out in the love of his kind;

XV.

Spring and Summer and Autumn and Winter, and
all these old revolutions of earth;
All new-old revolutions of Empire—change of the
tide—what is all of it worth?

XVI.

What the philosophies, all the sciences, poesy, vary-
ing voices of prayer?
All that is noblest, all that is basest, all that is filthy
with all that is fair?

XVII.

What is it all, if we all of us end but in being our
own corpse-coffins at last,
Swallow'd in Vastness, lost in Silence, drown'd in
the deeps of a meaningless Past?

XVIII.

What but a murmur of gnats in the gloom, or a moment's anger of bees in their hive?—

  * * * *

Peace, let it be! for I loved him, and love him for ever: the dead are not dead but alive.

Dedicated to the Hon. J. Russell Lowell.

THE RING.

MIRIAM AND HER FATHER.

MIRIAM (*singing*).

MELLOW moon of heaven,
Bright in blue,
Moon of married hearts,
Hear me, you!

Twelve times in the year
　　Bring me bliss,
Globing Honey Moons
　　Bright as this.

Moon, you fade at times
　　From the night.
Young again you grow
　　Out of sight.

Silver crescent-curve,
　　Coming soon,
Globe again, and make
　　Honey Moon.

Shall not *my* love last,
　　Moon, with you,
For ten thousand years
　　Old and new?

FATHER.

And who was he with such love-drunken eyes
They made a thousand honey moons of one?

MIRIAM.

The prophet of his own, my Hubert—his
The words, and mine the setting. 'Air and
   Words,'
Said Hubert, when I sang the song, 'are bride
And bridegroom.' Does it please you?

FATHER.
                          Mainly, child,
Because I hear your Mother's voice in yours.
She——, why, you shiver tho' the wind is west
With all the warmth of summer.

MIRIAM.
          Well, I felt
On a sudden I know not what, a breath that past
With all the cold of winter.

FATHER (*muttering to himself*).
          Even so.
The Ghost in Man, the Ghost that once was Man,
But cannot wholly free itself from Man,
Are calling to each other thro' a dawn
Stranger than earth has ever seen; the veil
Is rending, and the Voices of the day
Are heard across the Voices of the dark.
No sudden heaven, nor sudden hell, for man,
But thro' the Will of One who knows and rules—
And utter knowledge is but utter love—
Æonian Evolution, swift or slow,

Thro' all the Spheres—an ever opening height,
An ever lessening earth—and she perhaps,
My Miriam, breaks her latest earthly link
With me to-day.

MIRIAM.

You speak so low, what is it?
Your 'Miriam breaks'—is making a new link
Breaking an old one?

FATHER.

No, for we, my child,
Have been till now each other's all-in-all.

MIRIAM.

And you the lifelong guardian of the child.

FATHER.

I, and one other whom you have not known.

MIRIAM.

And who? what other?

FATHER.

Whither are you bound?
For Naples which we only left in May?

MIRIAM.

No! father, Spain, but Hubert brings me home
With April and the swallow. Wish me joy!

FATHER.

What need to wish when Hubert weds in you
The heart of Love, and you the soul of Truth
In Hubert?

MIRIAM.

Tho' you used to call me once
The lonely maiden-Princess of the wood,

Who meant to sleep her hundred summers out
Before a kiss should wake her.

FATHER.

Ay, but now
Your fairy Prince has found you, take this ring.

MIRIAM.

'Io t'amo'—and these diamonds—beautiful!
'From Walter,' and for me from you then?

FATHER.

Well,
One way for Miriam.

MIRIAM.

Miriam am I not?

Father.

This ring bequeath'd you by your mother, child,
Was to be given you—such her dying wish—
Given on the morning when you came of age
Or on the day you married. Both the days
Now close in one. The ring is doubly yours.
Why do you look so gravely at the tower?

Miriam.

I never saw it yet so all ablaze
With creepers crimsoning to the pinnacles,
As if perpetual sunset linger'd there,
And all ablaze too in the lake below!
And how the birds that circle round the tower
Are cheeping to each other of their flight
To summer lands!

FATHER.

      And that has made you grave?
Fly—care not. Birds and brides must leave the
    nest.
Child, I am happier in your happiness
Than in mine own.

MIRIAM.

            It is not that!

FATHER.

              What else?

MIRIAM.

That chamber in the tower.

FATHER.

           What chamber, child?
Your nurse is here?

MIRIAM.

My Mother's nurse and mine.
She comes to dress me in my bridal veil.

FATHER.

What did she say?

MIRIAM.

She said, that you and I
Had been abroad for my poor health so long
She fear'd I had forgotten her, and I ask'd
About my Mother, and she said, 'Thy hair
Is golden like thy Mother's, not so fine.'

FATHER.

What then? what more?

MIRIAM.

        She said—perhaps indeed
She wander'd, having wander'd now so far
Beyond the common date of death—that you,
When I was smaller than the statuette
Of my dear Mother on your bracket here—
You took me to that chamber in the tower,
The topmost—a chest there, by which you knelt—
And there were books and dresses—left to me,
A ring too which you kiss'd, and I, she said,
I babbled, Mother, Mother—as I used
To prattle to her picture—stretch'd my hands
As if I saw her; then a woman came
And caught me from my nurse. I hear her yet—
A sound of anger like a distant storm.

FATHER.
Garrulous old crone.

Miriam.

Poor nurse!

Father.

I bad her keep,
Like a seal'd book, all mention of the ring,
For I myself would tell you all to-day.

Miriam.

'She too might speak to-day,' she mumbled. Still,
I scarce have learnt the title of your book,
But you will turn the pages.

Father.

Ay, to-day!
I brought you to that chamber on your third

September birthday with your nurse, and felt

An icy breath play on me, while I stoopt

To take and kiss the ring.

MIRIAM.

      This very ring

Io t'amo?

FATHER.

     Yes, for some wild hope was mine

That, in the misery of my married life,

Miriam your Mother might appear to me.

She came to you, not me. The storm, you hear

Far-off, is Muriel—your step-mother's voice.

MIRIAM.

Vext, that you thought my Mother came to me?

Or at my crying 'Mother?' or to find

My Mother's diamonds hidden from her there,

Like worldly beauties in the Cell, not shown

To dazzle all that see them?

FATHER.

Wait a while.

Your Mother and step-mother—Miriam Erne

And Muriel Erne—the two were cousins—lived

With Muriel's mother on the down, that sees

A thousand squares of corn and meadow, far

As the gray deep, a landscape which your eyes

Have many a time ranged over when a babe.

MIRIAM.

I climb'd the hill with Hubert yesterday,

And from the thousand squares, one silent voice

Came on the wind, and seem'd to say 'Again.'

We saw far off an old forsaken house,

Then home, and past the ruin'd mill.

FATHER.

                                    And there
I found these cousins often by the brook,

For Miriam sketch'd and Muriel threw the fly;

The girls of equal age, but one was fair,

And one was dark, and both were beautiful.

No voice for either spoke within my heart

Then, for the surface eye, that only doats

On outward beauty, glancing from the one

To the other, knew not that which pleased it most,

The raven ringlet or the gold; but both

Were dowerless, and myself, I used to walk

This Terrace—morbid, melancholy; mine

And yet not mine the hall, the farm, the field;

For all that ample woodland whisper'd 'debt,'
The brook that feeds this lakelet murmur'd 'debt,'
And in yon arching avenue of old elms,
Tho' mine, not mine, I heard the sober rook
And carrion crow cry 'Mortgage.'

MIRIAM.

       Father's fault
Visited on the children!

FATHER.

       Ay, but then
A kinsman, dying, summon'd me to Rome—
He left me wealth—and while I journey'd hence,
And saw the world fly by me like a dream,
And while I communed with my truest self,
I woke to all of truest in myself,

Till, in the gleam of those mid-summer dawns,

The form of Muriel faded, and the face

Of Miriam grew upon me, till I knew;

And past and future mix'd in Heaven and made

The rosy twilight of a perfect day.

Miriam.

So glad? no tear for him, who left you wealth,

Your kinsman?

Father.

     I had seen the man but once;

He loved my name not me; and then I pass'd

Home, and thro' Venice, where a jeweller,

So far gone down, or so far up in life,

That he was nearing his own hundred, sold

This ring to me, then laugh'd 'the ring is weird.'

And weird and worn and wizard-like was he.

'Why weird?' I ask'd him; and he said 'The souls

Of two repentant Lovers guard the ring;'

Then with a ribald twinkle in his bleak eyes—

'And if you give the ring to any maid,

They still remember what it cost them here,

And bind the maid to love you by the ring;

And if the ring were stolen from the maid,

The theft were death or madness to the thief,

So sacred those Ghost Lovers hold the gift.'

And then he told their legend:

      'Long ago

Two lovers parted by a scurrilous tale

Had quarrell'd, till the man repenting sent

This ring "Io t'amo" to his best beloved,

And sent it on her birthday. She in wrath

Return'd it on her birthday, and that day
His death-day, when, half-frenzied by the ring,
He wildly fought a rival suitor, him
The causer of that scandal, fought and fell;
And she that came to part them all too late,
And found a corpse and silence, drew the ring
From his dead finger, wore it till her death,
Shrined him within the temple of her heart,
Made every moment of her after life
A virgin victim to his memory,
And dying rose, and rear'd her arms, and cried
"I see him, Io t'amo, Io t'amo."'

MIRIAM.

Legend or true? so tender should be true!
Did *he* believe it? did you ask him?

FATHER.
                        Ay!
But that half skeleton, like a barren ghost
From out the fleshless world of spirits, laugh'd:
A hollow laughter!

MIRIAM.
                    Vile, so near the ghost
Himself, to laugh at love in death! But you?

FATHER.
Well, as the bygone lover thro' this ring
Had sent his cry for her forgiveness, I
Would call thro' this 'Io t'amo' to the heart
Of Miriam; then I bad the man engrave
'From Walter' on the ring, and send it—wrote
Name, surname, all as clear as noon, but he—
Some younger hand must have engraven the ring—

His fingers were so stiffen'd by the frost
Of seven and ninety winters, that he scrawl'd
A 'Miriam' that might seem a 'Muriel';
And Muriel claim'd and open'd what I meant
For Miriam, took the ring, and flaunted it
Before that other whom I loved and love.'

  A mountain stay'd me here, a minster there,
A galleried palace, or a battlefield,
Where stood the sheaf of Peace : but—coming home—
And on your Mother's birthday—all but yours—
A week betwixt—and when the tower as now
Was all ablaze with crimson to the roof,
And all ablaze too plunging in the lake
Head-foremost—who were those that stood between
The tower and that rich phantom of the tower?
Muriel and Miriam, each in white, and like
May-blossoms in mid autumn—was it they?

A light shot upward on them from the lake.
What sparkled there? whose hand was that? they
      stood
So close together.   I am not keen of sight,
But coming nearer—Muriel had the ring—
'O Miriam! have you given your ring to her?
O Miriam!' Miriam redden'd, Muriel clench'd
The hand that wore it, till I cried again:
'O Miriam, if you love me take the ring!'
She glanced at me, at Muriel, and was mute.
'Nay, if you cannot love me, let it be.'
Then—Muriel standing ever statue-like—
She turn'd, and in her soft imperial way
And saying gently: 'Muriel, by your leave,'
Unclosed the hand, and from it drew the ring,
And gave it me, who pass'd it down her own,
'Io t'amo, all is well then.' Muriel fled.

MIRIAM.

Poor Muriel!

FATHER.

    Ay, poor Muriel when you hear
What follows!   Miriam loved me from the first,
Not thro' the ring; but on her marriage-morn
This birthday, death-day, and betrothal ring,
Laid on her table overnight, was gone;
And after hours of search and doubt and threats,
And hubbub, Muriel enter'd with it, 'See!—
Found in a chink of that old moulder'd floor!'
My Miriam nodded with a pitying smile,
As who should say 'that those who lose can find.'
 Then I and she were married for a year,
One year without a storm, or even a cloud;

And you my Miriam born within the year;

And she my Miriam dead within the year.

   I sat beside her dying, and she gaspt:

'The books, the miniature, the lace are hers,

My ring too when she comes of age, or when

She marries; you—you loved me, kept your word.

You love me still " Io t'amo."—Muriel—no—

She cannot love; she loves her own hard self,

Her firm will, her fix'd purpose. Promise me,

Miriam not Muriel—she shall have the ring.'

And there the light of other life, which lives

Beyond our burial and our buried eyes,

Gleam'd for a moment in her own on earth.

I swore the vow, then with my latest kiss

Upon them, closed her eyes, which would not close,

But kept their watch upon the ring and you.

Your birthday was her death-day.

MIRIAM.

                    O poor Mother!
And you, poor desolate Father, and poor me,
The little senseless, worthless, wordless babe,
Saved when your life was wreck'd!

FATHER.

                         Desolate? yes!
Desolate as that sailor, whom the storm
Had parted from his comrade in the boat,
And dash'd half dead on barren sands, was I.
Nay, you were my one solace; only—you
Were always ailing. Muriel's mother sent,
And sure am I, by Muriel, one day came
And saw you, shook her head, and patted yours,
And smiled, and making with a kindly pinch
Each poor pale cheek a momentary rose—

'*That* should be fix'd,' she said; 'your pretty bud,
So blighted here, would flower into full health
Among our heath and bracken. Let her come!
And we will feed her with our mountain air,
And send her home to you rejoicing.' No—
We could not part. And once, when you my girl
Rode on my shoulder home—the tiny fist
Had graspt a daisy from your Mother's grave—
By the lych-gate was Muriel. 'Ay,' she said,
'Among the tombs in this damp vale of yours!
You scorn my Mother's warning, but the child
Is paler than before. We often walk
In open sun, and see beneath our feet
The mist of autumn gather from your lake,
And shroud the tower; and once we only saw
Your gilded vane, a light above the mist'—
(Our old bright bird that still is veering there

Above his four gold letters) 'and the light,'

She said, 'was like that light'—and there she paused,

And long; till I believing that the girl's

Lean fancy, groping for it, could not find

One likeness, laugh'd a little and found her two—

'A warrior's crest above the cloud of war'—

'A fiery phœnix rising from the smoke,

The pyre he burnt in.'—'Nay,' she said, 'the light

That glimmers on the marsh and on the grave.'

And spoke no more, but turn'd and pass'd away.

 Miriam, I am not surely one of those

Caught by the flower that closes on the fly,

But after ten slow weeks her fix'd intent,

In aiming at an all but hopeless mark

To strike it, struck; I took, I left you there;

I came, I went, was happier day by day;

For Muriel nursed you with a mother's care;

Till on that clear and heather-scented height

The rounder cheek had brighten'd into bloom.

She always came to meet me carrying you,

And all her talk was of the babe she loved;

So, following her old pastime of the brook,

She threw the fly for me; but oftener left

That angling to the mother. 'Muriel's health

Had weaken'd, nursing little Miriam. Strange!

She used to shun the wailing babe, and doats

On this of yours.' But when the matron saw

That hinted love was only wasted bait,

Not risen to, she was bolder. 'Ever since

You sent the fatal ring'—I told her 'sent

To Miriam,' 'Doubtless—ay, but ever since

In all the world my dear one sees but you—

In your sweet babe she finds but you—she makes

Her heart a mirror that reflects but you.'
And then the tear fell, the voice broke. *Her
heart!*
I gazed into the mirror, as a man
Who sees his face in water, and a stone,
That glances from the bottom of the pool,
Strike upward thro' the shadow; yet at last,
Gratitude—loneliness—desire to keep
So skilled a nurse about you always—nay!
Some half remorseful kind of pity too—
Well! well, you know I married Muriel Erne.

'I take thee Muriel for my wedded wife'—
I had forgotten it was your birthday, child—
When all at once with some electric thrill
A cold air pass'd between us, and the hands
Fell from each other, and were join'd again.

No second cloudless honeymoon was mine.

For by and by she sicken'd of the farce,

She dropt the gracious mask of motherhood,

She came no more to meet me, carrying you,

Nor ever cared to set you on her knee,

Nor ever let you gambol in her sight,

Nor ever cheer'd you with a kindly smile,

Nor ever ceased to clamour for the ring;

Why had I sent the ring at first to her?

Why had I made her love me thro' the ring,

And then had changed? so fickle are men—the
    best!

Not she—but now my love was hers again,

The ring by right, she said, was hers again.

At times too shrilling in her angrier moods,

'That weak and watery nature love you? No!

"*Io* t'amo, *Io* t'amo"!' flung herself

Against my heart, but often while her lips

Were warm upon my cheek, an icy breath,
As from the grating of a sepulchre,
Past over both. I told her of my vow,
No pliable idiot I to break my vow;
But still she made her outcry for the ring;
For one monotonous fancy madden'd her,
Till I myself was madden'd with her cry,
And even that 'Io t'amo,' those three sweet
Italian words, became a weariness.

   My people too were scared with eerie sounds,
A footstep, a low throbbing in the walls,
A noise of falling weights that never fell,
Weird whispers, bells that rang without a hand,
Door-handles turn'd when none was at the door,
And bolted doors that open'd of themselves:
And one betwixt the dark and light had seen
Her, bending by the cradle of her babe.

MIRIAM.

And I remember once that being waked
By noises in the house—and no one near—
I cried for nurse, and felt a gentle hand
Fall on my forehead, and a sudden face
Look'd in upon me like a gleam and pass'd,
And I was quieted, and slept again.
Or is it some half memory of a dream?

FATHER.

Your fifth September birthday.

MIRIAM.

      And the face,
The hand,—my Mother.

FATHER.

      Miriam, on that day
Two lovers parted by no scurrilous tale—
Mere want of gold—and still for twenty years
Bound by the golden cord of their first love—
Had ask'd us to their marriage, and to share
Their marriage-banquet. Muriel, paler then
Than ever you were in your cradle, moan'd,
'I am fitter for my bed, or for my grave,
I cannot go, go you.' And then she rose,
She clung to me with such a hard embrace,
So lingeringly long, that half-amazed
I parted from her, and I went alone.
And when the bridegroom murmur'd, 'With this
  ring,'
I felt for what I could not find, the key,
The guardian of her relics, of *her* ring.

I kept it as a sacred amulet

About me,—gone! and gone in that embrace!

Then, hurrying home, I found her not in house

Or garden—up the tower—an icy air

Fled by me.—There, the chest was open—all

The sacred relics tost about the floor—

Among them Muriel lying on her face—

I raised her, call'd her 'Muriel, Muriel wake!'

The fatal ring lay near her; the glazed eye

Glared at me as in horror. Dead! I took

And chafed the freezing hand. A red mark ran

All round one finger pointed straight, the rest

Were crumpled inwards. Dead!—and maybe stung

With some remorse, had stolen, worn the ring—

Then torn it from her finger, or as if—

For never had I seen her show remorse—

As if—

MIRIAM.

—those two Ghost lovers—

FATHER.

Lovers yet—

MIRIAM.

Yes, yes!

FATHER.

—but dead so long, gone up so far,
That now their ever-rising life has dwarf'd
Or lost the moment of their past on earth,
As we forget our wail at being born.
As if—

MIRIAM.

a dearer ghost had—

Father.

                              —wrench'd it away.

Miriam.

Had floated in with sad reproachful eyes,
Till from her own hand she had torn the ring
In fright, and fallen dead.   And I myself
Am half afraid to wear it.

Father.

                        Well, no more!
No bridal music this! but fear not you!
You have the ring she guarded; that poor link
With earth is broken, and has left her free,
Except that, still drawn downward for an hour,
Her spirit hovering by the church, where she

Was married too, may linger, till she sees
Her maiden coming like a Queen, who leaves
Some colder province in the North to gain
Her capital city, where the loyal bells
Clash welcome—linger, till her own, the babe
She lean'd to from her Spiritual sphere,
Her lonely maiden-Princess, crown'd with flowers,
Has enter'd on the larger woman-world
Of wives and mothers.

       But the bridal veil—
Your nurse is waiting. Kiss me child and go.

FORLORN.

I.

' HE is fled—I wish him dead—

He that wrought my ruin—

O the flattery and the craft

Which were my undoing . . .

In the night, in the night,

When the storms are blowing.

II.

' Who was witness of the crime?

Who shall now reveal it?

He is fled, or he is dead,
    Marriage will conceal it . . .
In the night, in the night,
    While the gloom is growing.'

III.

Catherine, Catherine, in the night
    What is this you're dreaming?
There is laughter down in Hell
    At your simple scheming . . .
    In the night, in the night,
    When the ghosts are fleeting.

IV.

You to place a hand in his
    Like an honest woman's,

You that lie with wasted lungs

    Waiting for your summons . . .

    In the night, O the night!

    O the deathwatch beating!

v.

There will come a witness soon

    Hard to be confuted,

All the world will hear a voice

    Scream you are polluted . . .

    In the night! O the night,

    When the owls are wailing!

vi.

Shame and marriage, Shame and marriage,

    Fright and foul dissembling,

Bantering bridesman, reddening priest,
　Tower and altar trembling . . .
　In the night, O the night,
　When the mind is failing!

VII.

Mother, dare you kill your child?
　How your hand is shaking!
Daughter of the seed of Cain,
　What is this you're taking? . . .
　In the night, O the night,
　While the house is sleeping.

VIII.

Dreadful! has it come to this,
　O unhappy creature?

You that would not tread on a worm

    For your gentle nature . . .

    In the night, O the night,

    O the night of weeping!

IX.

Murder would not veil your sin,

    Marriage will not hide it,

Earth and Hell will brand your name,

    Wretch you must abide it . . .

    In the night, O the night,

    Long before the dawning.

X.

Up, get up, and tell him all,

    Tell him you were lying!

Do not die with a lie in your mouth,
    You that know you're dying . . .
In the night, O the night,
    While the grave is yawning.

XI.

No—you will not die before,
    Tho' you'll ne'er be stronger;
You will live till *that* is born,
    Then a little longer . . .
In the night, O the night,
    While the Fiend is prowling.

XII.

Death and marriage, Death and marriage!
    Funeral hearses rolling!

Black with bridal favours mixt!
    Bridal bells with tolling! . . .
    In the night, O the night,
    When the wolves are howling.

XIII.

Up, get up, the time is short,
    Tell him now or never!
Tell him all before you die,
    Lest you die for ever . . .
    In the night, O the night,
    Where there's no forgetting.

XIV.

Up she got, and wrote him all,
    All her tale of sadness,

Blister'd every word with tears,

    And eased her heart of madness . . .

In the night, and nigh the dawn,

    And while the moon was setting.

HAPPY.

THE LEPER'S BRIDE.

I.

Why wail you, pretty plover? and what is it that you fear?
Is he sick your mate like mine? have you lost him, is he fled?
And there—the heron rises from his watch beside the mere,
And flies above the leper's hut, where lives the living-dead.

II.

Come back, nor let me know it! would he live and
    die alone?
  And has he not forgiven me yet, his over-jealous
    bride,
Who am, and was, and will be his, his own and only
    own,
  To share his living death with him, die with him
    side by side?

III.

Is that the leper's hut on the solitary moor,
  Where noble Ulric dwells forlorn, and wears the
    leper's weed?
The door is open. He! is he standing at the door,
  My soldier of the Cross? it is he and he indeed!

IV.

My roses—will he take them *now*—mine, his—
　from off the tree
　We planted both together, happy in our marriage
　　morn?
O God, I could blaspheme, for he fought Thy fight
　for Thee,
　And Thou hast made him leper to compass him
　　with scorn—

V.

Hast spared the flesh of thousands, the coward and
　the base,
　And set a crueller mark than Cain's on him, the
　　good and brave!
He sees me, waves me from him. I will front him
　face to face.

You need not wave me from you. I would leap
into your grave.

  *   *   *   *

VI.

My warrior of the Holy Cross and of the conquering sword,
 The roses that you cast aside—once more I bring you these.
No nearer? do you scorn me when you tell me O my lord,
 You would not mar the beauty of your bride with your disease.

VII.

You say your body is so foul—then here I stand apart,

Who yearn to lay my loving head upon your leprous breast.
The leper plague may scale my skin but never taint my heart;
Your body is not foul to me, and body is foul at best.

VIII.

I loved you first when young and fair, but now I love you most;
The fairest flesh at last is filth on which the worm will feast;
This poor rib-grated dungeon of the holy human ghost,
This house with all its hateful needs no cleaner than the beast,

IX.

This coarse diseaseful creature which in Eden was divine,
  This Satan-haunted ruin, this little city of sewers,
This wall of solid flesh that comes between your soul and mine,
  Will vanish and give place to the beauty that endures,

X.

The beauty that endures on the Spiritual height,
  When we shall stand transfigured, like Christ on Hermon hill,
And moving each to music, soul in soul and light in light,
  Shall flash thro' one another in a moment as we will.

XI.

Foul! foul! the word was yours not mine, I worship that right hand
  Which fell'd the foes before you as the woodman fells the wood,
And sway'd the sword that lighten'd back the sun of Holy land,
  And clove the Moslem crescent moon, and changed it into blood.

XII.

And once I worshipt all too well this creature of decay,
  For Age will chink the face, and Death will freeze the supplest limbs—
Yet you in your mid manhood—O the grief when yesterday

They bore the Cross before you to the chant of funeral hymns.

XIII.

'Libera me, Domine!' you sang the Psalm, and when
The Priest pronounced you dead, and flung the mould upon your feet,
A beauty came upon your face, not that of living men,
But seen upon the silent brow when life has ceased to beat.

XIV.

'Libera *nos*, Domine'—you knew not one was there
Who saw you kneel beside your bier, and weeping scarce could see;

May I come a little nearer, I that heard, and changed the prayer

And sang the married 'nos' for the solitary 'me.'

XV.

My beauty marred by you? by you! so be it. All is well

If I lose it and myself in the higher beauty, yours.

My beauty lured that falcon from his eyry on the fell,

Who never caught one gleam of the beauty which endures—

XVI.

The Count who sought to snap the bond that link'd us life to life,

Who whisper'd me 'your Ulric loves'—a little nearer still—

He hiss'd, 'Let us revenge ourselves, your Ulric
  woos my wife'—
A lie by which he thought he could subdue me
  to his will.

XVII.

I knew that you were near me when I let him kiss
  my brow;
Well, he kiss'd me on the lips, I was jealous,
  anger'd, vain,
And I meant to make *you* jealous. Are you
  jealous of me now?
Your pardon, O my love, if I ever gave you pain.

XVIII.

You never once accused me, but I wept alone, and
  sigh'd

In the winter of the Present for the summer of
the Past;
That icy winter silence—how it froze you from
your bride,
Tho' I made one barren effort to break it at
the last.

XIX.

I brought you, you remember, these roses, when I
knew
You were parting for the war, and you took them
tho' you frown'd;
You frown'd and yet you kiss'd them. All at
once the trumpet blew,
And you spurr'd your fiery horse, and you hurl'd
them to the ground.

XX.

You parted for the Holy War without a word to me,
And clear myself unask'd—not I. My nature was too proud.
And him I saw but once again, and far away was he,
When I was praying in a storm—the crash was long and loud—

XXI.

That God would ever slant His bolt from falling on your head—
Then I lifted up my eyes, he was coming down the fell—
I clapt my hands. The sudden fire from Heaven had dash'd him dead,
And sent him charr'd and blasted to the deathless fire of Hell.

XXII.

See, I sinn'd but for a moment. I repented and
     repent,
  And trust myself forgiven by the God to whom
     I kneel.
A little nearer? Yes. I shall hardly be content
  Till I be leper like yourself, my love, from head
     to heel.

XXIII.

O foolish dreams, that you, that I, would slight our
     marriage oath :
  I held you at that moment even dearer than
     before ;
Now God has made you leper in His loving care
     for both,

That we might cling together, never doubt each
>other more.

XXIV.

The Priest, who join'd you to the dead, has join'd
>our hands of old;
>If man and wife be but one flesh, let mine be
>>leprous too,
>As dead from all the human race as if beneath the
>>mould;
>If you be dead, then I am dead, who only live
>>for you.

XXV.

Would Earth tho' hid in cloud not be follow'd by
>the Moon?
>The leech forsake the dying bed for terror of
>his life?

The shadow leave the Substance in the brooding
light of noon?
Or if *I* had been the leper would you have left
the wife?

XXVI.

Not take them? Still you wave me off—poor roses
—must I go—
I have worn them year by year—from the bush
we both had set—
What? fling them to you?—well—that were hardly
gracious. No!
Your plague but passes by the touch. A little
nearer yet!

XXVII.

There, there! he buried you, the Priest; the Priest
is not to blame,

He joins us once again, to his either office true:
I thank him.   I am happy, happy.   Kiss me.   In the name
Of the everlasting God, I will live and die with you.

[DEAN MILMAN has remarked that the protection and care afforded by the Church to this blighted race of lepers was among the most beautiful of its offices during the Middle Ages. The leprosy of the thirteenth and fourteenth centuries was supposed to be a legacy of the crusades, but was in all probability the offspring of meagre and unwholesome diet, miserable lodging and clothing, physical and moral degradation. The services of the Church in the seclusion of these unhappy sufferers were most affecting. The stern duty of looking to the public welfare is tempered with exquisite compassion for the victims of this loathsome disease. The ritual for the sequestration of the leprous differed little from the burial service. After the leper had been sprinkled with holy water, the priest conducted him into the church, the leper singing the psalm 'Libera me domine,' and the crucifix and bearer going before. In the church a black cloth was stretched over two trestles in front of the altar, and the leper leaning at its side devoutly heard mass. The priest, taking up a little earth in his cloak, threw it on one of the leper's feet, and put him out of the church, if it did not rain too heavily; took him to his hut in the midst of the fields, and then uttered the prohibitions: 'I forbid you entering the church . . . . or entering the company of others. I forbid you quitting your home without your leper's dress.' He concluded: 'Take this dress, and wear it in token of humility; take these gloves, take this clapper, as a sign that you are forbidden to speak to any one. You are not to be indignant at being thus separated from others, and as to your little wants, good people will provide for you, and God will not desert you.' Then in this old ritual follow these sad words: 'When it shall come to pass that the leper shall pass out of this world, he shall be buried in his hut, and not in the churchyard.' At first there was a doubt whether wives should follow their husbands who had been leprous, or remain in the world and marry again. The Church decided that the marriage-tie was indissoluble, and so bestowed on these unhappy beings this immense source of consolation.

With a love stronger than this living death, lepers were followed into banishment from the haunts of men by their faithful wives. Readers of Sir J. Stephen's *Essays on Ecclesiastical Biography* will recollect the description of the founder of the Franciscan order, how, controlling his involuntary disgust, St. Francis of Assisi washed the feet and dressed the sores of the lepers, once at least reverently applying his lips to their wounds.—BOUCHER-JAMES.]

This ceremony of *quasi*-burial varied considerably at different times and in different places. In some cases a grave was dug, and the leper's face was often covered during the service.

TO ULYSSES.

I.

Ulysses, much-experienced man,
    Whose eyes have known this globe of ours,
    Her tribes of men, and trees, and flowers,
From Corrientes to Japan,

II.

To you that bask below the Line,
    I soaking here in winter wet—
    The century's three strong eights have met
To drag me down to seventy-nine

III.

In summer if I reach my day—
>   To you, yet young, who breathe the balm
>   Of summer-winters by the palm
And orange grove of Paraguay,

IV.

I tolerant of the colder time,
>   Who love the winter woods, to trace
>   On paler heavens the branching grace
Of leafless elm, or naked lime,

V.

And see my cedar green, and there
>   My giant ilex keeping leaf
>   When frost is keen and days are brief—
Or marvel how in English air

VI.

My yucca, which no winter quells,
    Altho' the months have scarce begun,
    Has push'd toward our faintest sun
A spike of half-accomplish'd bells—

VII.

Or watch the waving pine which here
    The warrior of Caprera set,[1]
    A name that earth will not forget
Till earth has roll'd her latest year—

VIII.

I, once half-crazed for larger light
    On broader zones beyond the foam,
    But chaining fancy now at home
Among the quarried downs of Wight,

IX.

Not less would yield full thanks to you
    For your rich gift, your tale of lands
    I know not,[2] your Arabian sands;
Your cane, your palm, tree-fern, bamboo,

X.

The wealth of tropic bower and brake;
    Your Oriental Eden-isles,[3]
    Where man, nor only Nature smiles;
Your wonder of the boiling lake;[4]

XI.

Phra-Chai, the Shadow of the Best,[5]
    Phra-bat[6] the step; your Pontic coast;
    Crag-cloister;[7] Anatolian Ghost;[8]
Hong-Kong,[9] Karnac,[10] and all the rest.

XII.

Thro' which I follow'd line by line
    Your leading hand, and came, my friend,
    To prize your various book, and send
A gift of slenderer value, mine.

NOTES TO ULYSSES.

'Ulysses,' the title of a number of essays by W. G. Palgrave. He died at Monte Video before seeing either this volume or my poem.

[1] Garibaldi said to me, alluding to his barren island, 'I wish I had your trees.'

[2] The tale of Nejd.

[3] The Philippines.

[4] In Dominica.

[5] The Shadow of the Lord. Certain obscure markings on a rock in Siam, which express the image of Budda to the Buddhist more or less distinctly according to his faith and his moral worth.

[6] The footstep of the Lord on another rock.

[7] The monastery of Sumelas.

[8] Anatolian Spectre stories.

[9] The three cities.

[10] Travels in Egypt.

TO MARY BOYLE.

WITH THE FOLLOWING POEM.

I.

'SPRING-FLOWERS'! While you still delay to take
    Your leave of Town,
Our elmtree's ruddy-hearted blossom-flake
    Is fluttering down.

II.

Be truer to your promise. There! I heard
    One cuckoo call.
Be needle to the magnet of your word,
    Nor wait, till all

III.

Our vernal bloom from every vale and plain
    And garden pass,
And all the gold from each laburnum chain
    Drop to the grass.

IV.

Is memory with your Marian gone to rest,
    Dead with the dead?
For ere she left us, when we met, you prest
    My hand, and said

V.

'I come with your spring-flowers.' You came not, friend;
    My birds would sing,
You heard not. Take then this spring-flower I send,
    This song of spring,

VI.

Found yesterday—forgotten mine own rhyme
    By mine old self,
As I shall be forgotten by old Time,
    Laid on the shelf—

VII.

A rhyme that flower'd betwixt the whitening sloe
    And kingcup blaze,
And more than half a hundred years ago,
    In rick-fire days,

VIII.

When Dives loathed the times, and paced his land
    In fear of worse,
And sanguine Lazarus felt a vacant hand
    Fill with *his* purse.

IX.

For lowly minds were madden'd to the height
    By tonguester tricks,
And once—I well remember that red night
    When thirty ricks,

X.

All flaming, made an English homestead Hell—
    These hands of mine
Have helpt to pass a bucket from the well
    Along the line,

XI.

When this bare dome had not begun to gleam
    Thro' youthful curls,
And you were then a lover's fairy dream,
    His girl of girls;

XII.

And you, that now are lonely, and with Grief
    Sit face to face,
Might find a flickering glimmer of relief
    In change of place.

XIII.

What use to brood? this life of mingled pains
    And joys to me,
Despite of every Faith and Creed, remains
    The Mystery.

XIV.

Let golden youth bewail the friend, the wife,
    For ever gone.
He dreams of that long walk thro' desert life
    Without the one.

XV.

The silver year should cease to mourn and sigh—
    Not long to wait—
So close are we, dear Mary, you and I
    To that dim gate.

XVI

Take, read! and be the faults your Poet makes
    Or many or few,
He rests content, if his young music wakes
    A wish in you

XVII.

To change our dark Queen-city, all her realm
    Of sound and smoke,
For his clear heaven, and these few lanes of elm
    And whispering oak.

THE PROGRESS OF SPRING.

I.

The groundflame of the crocus breaks the mould,
    Fair Spring slides hither o'er the Southern sea,
Wavers on her thin stem the snowdrop cold
    That trembles not to kisses of the bee:
Come Spring, for now from all the dripping eaves
    The spear of ice has wept itself away,
And hour by hour unfolding woodbine leaves
    O'er his uncertain shadow droops the day.
She comes! The loosen'd rivulets run;
    The frost-bead melts upon her golden hair;
Her mantle, slowly greening in the Sun,

Now wraps her close, now arching leaves her bare
To breaths of balmier air;

II.

Up leaps the lark, gone wild to welcome her,
    About her glance the tits, and shriek the jays,
Before her skims the jubilant woodpecker,
    The linnet's bosom blushes at her gaze,
While round her brows a woodland culver flits,
    Watching her large light eyes and gracious looks,
And in her open palm a halcyon sits
    Patient—the secret splendour of the brooks.
Come Spring! She comes on waste and wood,
    On farm and field: but enter also here,
Diffuse thyself at will thro' all my blood,
    And, tho' thy violet sicken into sere,
    Lodge with me all the year!

III.

Once more a downy drift against the brakes,
  Self-darken'd in the sky, descending slow!
But gladly see I thro' the wavering flakes
  Yon blanching apricot like snow in snow.
These will thine eyes not brook in forest-paths,
  On their perpetual pine, nor round the beech;
They fuse themselves to little spicy baths,
  Solved in the tender blushes of the peach;
They lose themselves and die
  On that new life that gems the hawthorn line;
Thy gay lent-lilies wave and put them by,
  And out once more in varnish'd glory shine
  Thy stars of celandine.

IV.

She floats across the hamlet.   Heaven lours,
   But in the tearful splendour of her smiles
I see the slowly-thickening chestnut towers
   Fill out the spaces by the barren tiles.
Now past her feet the swallow circling flies,
   A clamorous cuckoo stoops to meet her hand;
Her light makes rainbows in my closing eyes,
   I hear a charm of song thro' all the land.
Come, Spring!   She comes, and Earth is glad
   To roll her North below thy deepening dome,
But ere thy maiden birk be wholly clad,
   And these low bushes dip their twigs in foam,
     Make all true hearths thy home.

V.

Across my garden! and the thicket stirs,
  The fountain pulses high in sunnier jets,
The blackcap warbles, and the turtle purrs,
  The starling claps his tiny castanets.
Still round her forehead wheels the woodland dove,
  And scatters on her throat the sparks of dew,
The kingcup fills her footprint, and above
  Broaden the glowing isles of vernal blue.
Hail ample presence of a Queen,
  Bountiful, beautiful, apparell'd gay,
Whose mantle, every shade of glancing green,
  Flies back in fragrant breezes to display
  A tunic white as May!

VI

She whispers, 'From the South I bring you balm,
    For on a tropic mountain was I born,
While some dark dweller by the coco-palm
    Watch'd my far meadow zoned with airy morn;
From under rose a muffled moan of floods;
    I sat beneath a solitude of snow;
There no one came, the turf was fresh, the woods
    Plunged gulf on gulf thro' all their vales below.
I saw beyond their silent tops
    The steaming marshes of the scarlet cranes,
The slant seas leaning on the mangrove copse,
    And summer basking in the sultry plains
    About a land of canes;

VII.

'Then from my vapour-girdle soaring forth
　　I scaled the buoyant highway of the birds,
And drank the dews and drizzle of the North,
　　That I might mix with men, and hear their words
On pathway'd plains; for—while my hand exults
　　Within the bloodless heart of lowly flowers
To work old laws of Love to fresh results,
　　Thro' manifold effect of simple powers—
I too would teach the man
　　Beyond the darker hour to see the bright,
That his fresh life may close as it began,
　　The still-fulfilling promise of a light
　　　Narrowing the bounds of night.'

VIII.

So wed thee with my soul, that I may mark
    The coming year's great good and varied ills,
And new developments, whatever spark
    Be struck from out the clash of warring wills;
Or whether, since our nature cannot rest,
    The smoke of war's volcano burst again
From hoary deeps that belt the changeful West,
    Old Empires, dwellings of the kings of men;
Or should those fail, that hold the helm,
    While the long day of knowledge grows and warms,
And in the heart of this most ancient realm
    A hateful voice be utter'd, and alarms
    Sounding 'To arms! to arms!'

IX.

A simpler, saner lesson might he learn
    Who reads thy gradual process, Holy Spring.
Thy leaves possess the season in their turn,
    And in their time thy warblers rise on wing.
How surely glidest thou from March to May,
    And changest, breathing it, the sullen wind,
Thy scope of operation, day by day,
    Larger and fuller, like the human mind!
Thy warmths from bud to bud
    Accomplish that blind model in the seed,
And men have hopes, which race the restless blood,
    That after many changes may succeed
    Life, which is Life indeed.

MERLIN AND THE GLEAM.

I.

O young Mariner,

You from the haven

Under the sea-cliff,

You that are watching

The gray Magician

With eyes of wonder,

I am Merlin,

And *I* am dying,

I am Merlin

Who follow The Gleam.

II.

Mighty the Wizard

Who found me at sunrise

Sleeping, and woke me

And learn'd me Magic!

Great the Master,

And sweet the Magic,

When over the valley,

In early summers,

Over the mountain,

On human faces,

And all around me,

Moving to melody,

Floated The Gleam.

III.

Once at the croak of a Raven who
crost it,
A barbarous people,
Blind to the magic,
And deaf to the melody,
Snarl'd at and cursed me.
A demon vext me,
The light retreated,
The landskip darken'd,
The melody deaden'd,
The Master whisper'd
'Follow The Gleam.'

IV.

Then to the melody,

Over a wilderness

Gliding, and glancing at

Elf of the woodland,

Gnome of the cavern,

Griffin and Giant,

And dancing of Fairies

In desolate hollows,

And wraiths of the mountain,

And rolling of dragons

By warble of water,

Or cataract music

Of falling torrents,

Flitted The Gleam.

V.

Down from the mountain
And over the level,
And streaming and shining on
Silent river,
Silvery willow,
Pasture and plowland,
Horses and oxen,
Innocent maidens,
Garrulous children,
Homestead and harvest,
Reaper and gleaner,
And rough-ruddy faces
Of lowly labour,
Slided The Gleam.—

VI.

Then, with a melody

Stronger and statelier,

Led me at length

To the city and palace

Of Arthur the king;

Touch'd at the golden

Cross of the churches,

Flash'd on the Tournament,

Flicker'd and bicker'd

From helmet to helmet,

And last on the forehead

Of Arthur the blameless

Rested The Gleam.

VII.

Clouds and darkness

Closed upon Camelot;

Arthur had vanish'd

I knew not whither,

The king who loved me,

And cannot die;

For out of the darkness

Silent and slowly

The Gleam, that had waned to a wintry

    glimmer

On icy fallow

And faded forest,

Drew to the valley

Named of the shadow,

And slowly brightening

Out of the glimmer,

And slowly moving again to a melody

Yearningly tender,

Fell on the shadow,

No longer a shadow,

But clothed with The Gleam.

VIII.

And broader and brighter

The Gleam flying onward,

Wed to the melody,

Sang thro' the world;

And slower and fainter,

Old and weary,

But eager to follow,

I saw, whenever

In passing it glanced upon

Hamlet or city,

That under the Crosses

The dead man's garden,

The mortal hillock,

Would break into blossom;

And so to the land's

Last limit I came——

And can no longer,

But die rejoicing,

For thro' the Magic

Of Him the Mighty,

Who taught me in childhood,

There on the border

Of boundless Ocean,

And all but in Heaven

Hovers The Gleam.

IX.

Not of the sunlight,

Not of the moonlight,

Not of the starlight!

O young Mariner,

Down to the haven,

Call your companions,

Launch your vessel,

And crowd your canvas,

And, ere it vanishes

Over the margin,

After it, follow it,

Follow The Gleam.

ROMNEY'S REMORSE.

'I read Hayley's Life of Romney the other day—Romney wanted but education and reading to make him a very fine painter; but his ideal was not high nor fixed. How touching is the close of his life! He married at nineteen, and because Sir Joshua and others had said that "marriage spoilt an artist" almost immediately left his wife in the North and scarce saw her till the end of his life; when old, nearly mad and quite desolate, he went back to her and she received him and nursed him till he died. This quiet act of hers is worth all Romney's pictures! even as a matter of Art, I am sure.' (*Letters and Literary Remains of Edward Fitzgerald*, vol. i.)

'BEAT, little heart—I give you this and this'

Who are you? What! the Lady Hamilton?

Good, I am never weary painting you.

To sit once more? Cassandra, Hebe, Joan,

Or spinning at your wheel beside the vine—

Bacchante, what you will; and if I fail

To conjure and concentrate into form

And colour all you are, the fault is less

In me than Art. What Artist ever yet

Could make pure light live on the canvas? Art!

Why should I so disrelish that short word?

    Where am I? snow on all the hills! so hot,

So fever'd! never colt would more delight

To roll himself in meadow grass than I

To wallow in that winter of the hills.

    Nurse, were you hired? or came of your own will

To wait on one so broken, so forlorn?

Have I not met you somewhere long ago?

I am all but sure I have—in Kendal church—

O yes! I hired you for a season there,
And then we parted; but you look so kind
That you will not deny my sultry throat
One draught of icy water. There—you spill
The drops upon my forehead. Your hand shakes.
I am ashamed. I am a trouble to you,
Could kneel for your forgiveness. Are they tears?
For me—they do me too much grace—for me?
O Mary, Mary!

            Vexing you with words!
Words only, born of fever, or the fumes
Of that dark opiate dose you gave me,—words,
Wild babble. I have stumbled back again
Into the common day, the sounder self.
God stay me there, if only for your sake,
The truest, kindliest, noblest-hearted wife
That ever wore a Christian marriage-ring.

My curse upon the Master's apothegm,

That wife and children drag an Artist down!

This seem'd my lodestar in the Heaven of Art,

And lured me from the household fire on earth.

To you my days have been a life-long lie,

Grafted on half a truth, and tho' you say

'Take comfort, you have won the Painter's fame;

The best in me that sees the worst in me,

And groans to see it, finds no comfort there.

What fame? I am not Raphaël, Titian—no

Nor even a Sir Joshua, some will cry.

Wrong there! The painter's fame? but mine, that
    grew

Blown into glittering by the popular breath,

May float awhile beneath the sun, may roll

The rainbow hues of heaven about it—

                              There!

The colour'd bubble bursts above the abyss
Of Darkness, utter Lethe.

                                    Is it so?
Her sad eyes plead for my own fame with me
To make it dearer.

                        Look, the sun has risen
To flame along another dreary day.
Your hand.   How bright you keep your marriage-
    ring!
Raise me.   I thank you.

                             Has your opiate then
Bred this black mood? or am I conscious, more
Than other Masters, of the chasm between
Work and Ideal?   Or does the gloom of Age
And suffering cloud the height I stand upon

Even from myself? stand? stood . . . no more.

                                               And yet
The world would lose, if such a wife as you
Should vanish unrecorded. Might I crave
One favour? I am bankrupt of all claim
On your obedience, and my strongest wish
Falls flat before your least unwillingness.
Still would you—if it please you—sit to me?

    I dream'd last night of that clear summer noon,
When seated on a rock, and foot to foot
With your own shadow in the placid lake,
You claspt our infant daughter, heart to heart.
I had been among the hills, and brought you down
A length of staghorn-moss, and this you twined
About her cap. I see the picture yet,
Mother and child. A sound from far away,
No louder than a bee among the flowers,

A fall of water lull'd the noon asleep.

You still'd it for the moment with a song

Which often echo'd in me, while I stood

Before the great Madonna-masterpieces

Of ancient Art in Paris, or in Rome.

    Mary, my crayons! if I can, I will.

You should have been—I might have made you once,

Had I but known you as I know you now—

The true <u>Alcestis</u> of the time.   Your song—

Sit, listen!   I remember it, a proof

That I—even I—at times remember'd *you*.

    'Beat upon mine, little heart! beat, beat!

    Beat upon mine! you are mine, my sweet!

    All mine from your pretty blue eyes to your feet,

                   My sweet.'

Less profile! turn to me—three-quarter face.

'Sleep, little blossom, my honey, my bliss!

For I give you this, and I give you this!

And I blind your pretty blue eyes with a kiss!

      Sleep!'

Too early blinded by the kiss of death—

'Father and Mother will watch you grow'—

You watch'd, not I, she did not grow, she died.

'Father and Mother will watch you grow,

And gather the roses whenever they blow,

And find the white heather wherever you go,

      My sweet.'

Ah, my white heather only grows in heaven

With Milton's amaranth. There, there, there! a child

Had shamed me at it—Down, you idle tools,

Stampt into dust—tremulous, all awry,

Blurr'd like a landskip in a ruffled pool,—
Not one stroke firm. This Art, that harlot-like
Seduced me from you, leaves me harlot-like,
Who love her still, and whimper, impotent
To win her back before I die—and then—
Then, in the loud world's bastard judgment-day,
One truth will damn me with the mindless mob,
Who feel no touch of my temptation, more
More than all the myriad lies, that blacken round
The corpse of every man that gains a name;
'This model husband, this fine Artist'! Fool,
What matters? Six foot deep of burial mould
Will dull their comments! Ay, but when the shout
Of His descending peals from Heaven, and throbs
Thro' earth, and all her graves, if *He* should ask
'Why left you wife and children? for my sake,
According to my word?' and I replied

'Nay, Lord, for *Art*,' why, that would sound so mean
That all the dead, who wait the doom of Hell
For bolder sins than mine, adulteries,
Wife-murders,—nay, the ruthless Mussulman
Who flings his bowstrung Harem in the sea,
Would turn, and glare at me, and point and jeer,
And gibber at the worm, who, living, made
The wife of wives a widow-bride, and lost
Salvation for a sketch.

     I am wild again!
The coals of fire you heap upon my head
Have crazed me. Someone knocking there without?
No! Will my Indian brother come? to find
Me or my coffin? Should I know the man?
This worn-out Reason dying in her house

May leave the windows blinded, and if so,
Bid him farewell for me, and tell him—

         Hope!
I hear a death-bed Angel whisper 'Hope.'
"The miserable have no medicine
But only Hope!" He said it . . . in the play.
His crime was of the senses; of the mind
Mine; worse, cold, calculated.

         Tell my son—
O let me lean my head upon your breast.
'Beat little heart' on this fool brain of mine.
I once had friends—and many—none like you.
I love you more than when we married. Hope!
O yes, I hope, or fancy that, perhaps,
Human forgiveness touches heaven, and thence—
For you forgive me, you are sure of that—
Reflected, sends a light on the forgiven.

PARNASSUS.

> Exegi monumentum . . .
> Quod non . . .
> Possit diruere . . .
>   . . . innumerabilis
> Annorum series et fuga temporum.—HORACE.

I.

WHAT be those crown'd forms high over the sacred fountain?
Bards, that the mighty Muses have raised to the heights of the mountain,
And over the flight of the Ages! O Goddesses, help me up thither!

Lightning may shrivel the laurel of Cæsar, but mine would not wither.

Steep is the mountain, but you, you will help me to overcome it,

And stand with my head in the zenith, and roll my voice from the summit,

Sounding for ever and ever thro' Earth and her listening nations,

And mixt with the great Sphere-music of stars and of constellations.

.

II.

What be those two shapes high over the sacred fountain,

Taller than all the Muses, and huger than all the mountain?

On those two known peaks they stand ever spreading and heightening;
Poet, that evergreen laurel is blasted by more than lightning!
Look, in their deep double shadow the crown'd ones all disappearing!
Sing like a bird and be happy, nor hope for a deathless hearing!
'Sounding for ever and ever?' pass on! the sight confuses—
These are Astronomy and Geology, terrible Muses!

III.

If the lips were touch'd with fire from off a pure Pierian altar,

Tho' their music here be mortal need the singer greatly care?
Other songs for other worlds! the fire within him would not falter;
Let the golden Iliad vanish, Homer here is Homer there.

BY AN EVOLUTIONIST.

THE Lord let the house of a brute to the soul of a man,

And the man said 'Am I your debtor?'

And the Lord—'Not yet: but make it as clean as you can,

And then I will let you a better.'

I.

If my body come from brutes, my soul uncertain, or a fable,

Why not bask amid the senses while the sun of morning shines,
I, the finer brute rejoicing in my hounds, and in my stable,
Youth and Health, and birth and wealth, and choice of women and of wines?

II.

What hast thou done for me, grim Old Age, save breaking my bones on the rack?
Would I had past in the morning that looks so bright from afar!

OLD AGE.

Done for thee? starved the wild beast that was linkt with thee eighty years back.

Less weight now for the ladder-of-heaven that hangs on a star.

I.

If my body come from brutes, tho' somewhat finer than their own,

I am heir, and this my kingdom.   Shall the royal voice be mute?

No, but if the rebel subject seek to drag me from the throne,

Hold the sceptre, Human Soul, and rule thy Province of the brute.

II.

I have climb'd to the snows of Age, and I gaze at a field in the Past,

Where I sank with the body at times in the sloughs of a low desire,

But I hear no yelp of the beast, and the Man is quiet at last
As he stands on the heights of his life with a glimpse of a height that is higher.

FAR—FAR—AWAY.

(FOR MUSIC.)

WHAT sight so lured him thro' the fields he knew
As where earth's green stole into heaven's own hue,
>> Far—far—away?

What sound was dearest in his native dells?
The mellow lin-lan-lone of evening bells
>> Far—far—away.

What vague world-whisper, mystic pain or joy,
Thro' those three words would haunt him when a boy
>> Far—far—away?

A whisper from his dawn of life? a breath

From some fair dawn beyond the doors of death

    Far—far—away?

Far, far, how far? from o'er the gates of Birth,

The faint horizons, all the bounds of earth,

    Far—far—away?

What charm in words, a charm no words could give?

O dying words, can Music make you live

    Far—far—away?

POLITICS.

We move, the wheel must always move,
   Nor always on the plain,
And if we move to such a goal
   As Wisdom hopes to gain,
Then you that drive, and know your Craft,
   Will firmly hold the rein,
Nor lend an ear to random cries,
   Or you may drive in vain,
For some cry 'Quick' and some cry 'Slow,'
   But, while the hills remain,
Up hill 'Too-slow' will need the whip,
   Down hill 'Too-quick' the chain.

BEAUTIFUL CITY.

Beautiful city, the centre and crater of
  European confusion,
O you with your passionate shriek for the rights
  of an equal humanity,
How often your Re-volution has proven but
  E-volution
Roll'd again back on itself in the tides of
  a civic insanity!

THE ROSES ON THE TERRACE.

Rose, on this terrace fifty years ago,
    When I was in my June, you in your May,
Two words, '*My* Rose' set all your face aglow,
    And now that I am white, and you are gray,
That blush of fifty years ago, my dear,
    Blooms in the Past, but close to me to-day
As this red rose, which on our terrace here
    Glows in the blue of fifty miles away.

THE PLAY.

Act first, this Earth, a stage so gloom'd with woe
    You all but sicken at the shifting scenes.
And yet be patient. Our Playwright may show
    In some fifth Act what this wild Drama means.

ON ONE WHO AFFECTED AN EFFEMINATE MANNER.

While man and woman still are incomplete,
I prize that soul where man and woman meet,
Which types all Nature's male and female plan,
But, friend, man-woman is not woman-man.

TO ONE WHO RAN DOWN THE ENGLISH.

You make our faults too gross, and thence maintain

Our darker future.   May your fears be vain !

At times the small black fly upon the pane

May seem the black ox of the distant plain

THE SNOWDROP.

MANY, many welcomes

February fair-maid,

Ever as of old time,

Solitary firstling,

Coming in the cold time,

Prophet of the gay time,

Prophet of the May time,

Prophet of the roses,

Many, many welcomes

February fair-maid!

THE THROSTLE.

'Summer is coming, summer is coming.
    I know it, I know it, I know it.
Light again, leaf again, life again, love again,'
    Yes, my wild little Poet.

Sing the new year in under the blue.
    Last year you sang it as gladly.
'New, new, new, new'! Is it then *so* new
    That you should carol so madly?

'Love again, song again, nest again, young again'
    Never a prophet so crazy!

And hardly a daisy as yet, little friend,
See, there is hardly a daisy.

'Here again, here, here, here, happy year'!
O warble unchidden, unbidden!
Summer is coming, is coming, my dear,
And all the winters are hidden.

THE OAK.

Live thy Life,
    Young and old,
Like yon oak,
Bright in spring,
    Living gold;

Summer-rich
    Then; and then
Autumn-changed,
Soberer-hued
    Gold again.

All his leaves

    Fall'n at length,

Look, he stands,

Trunk and bough,

    Naked strength.

IN MEMORIAM.

W. G. WARD.

FAREWELL, whose like on earth I shall not find,
  Whose Faith and Work were bells of full accord,
My friend, the most unworldly of mankind,
  Most generous of all Ultramontanes, Ward,
How subtle at tierce and quart of mind with mind,
  How loyal in the following of thy Lord!

CROSSING THE BAR.

Sunset and evening star,
    And one clear call for me !
And may there be no moaning of the bar,
    When I put out to sea,

But such a tide as moving seems asleep,
    Too full for sound and foam,
When that which drew from out the boundless deep
    Turns again home.

Twilight and evening bell,
    And after that the dark !

And may there be no sadness of farewell,
    When I embark;

For tho' from out our bourne of Time and Place
    The flood may bear me far,
I hope to see my Pilot face to face
    When I have crost the bar.

THE END

Printed by R. & R. CLARK, *Edinburgh.*

www.ingramcontent.com/pod-product-compliance
Lightning Source LLC
Chambersburg PA
CBHW020247170426
43202CB00008B/265